The Advancement of Gemini Ai

Exploring New Features, Enhanced Integration, and Performance Upgrades of Gemini's Latest Innovations

Anthony R. Mullen

Copyright © Anthony R. Mullen, 2024. All rights reserved.

No part of this publication may be reproduced, distributed, or transmitted in any form or by any means, including photocopying, recording, or other electronic or mechanical methods, without the publisher's prior consent, except in the case of brief quotations embodied in critical reviews and certain other noncommercial users permitted by copyright law.

TABLE OF CONTENTS

Introduction 4

Chapter One: Gemini Live 13
    Free-Flowing Conversations with Gemini 13
    Hands-Free Operation and Background Use 16
    Availability: Rollout Schedule and Supported Platforms 19

Chapter Two: New Voice Options 22
    Selecting the Best Voice to Meet Your Needs 22
    Demonstration of Voice Features 25

Chapter Three: App Integration and Extensions 30
    Seamless Integration with Google Apps 30
    Managing Tasks with Gemini 33
    Keep and Tasks Integration 33
    YouTube Music Features 35
    Calendar Extension: Scheduling and Reminders ... 37

Chapter Four: Enhanced Android Integration 40
    Context-Aware Capabilities on Android 40
    Interacting with Content on Your Screen 43
    Drag-and-Drop Functionality 45

Chapter Five: Performance Improvements 50

The Advancement of Gemini AI

    Introduction of Gemini 1.5 Flash..............................50
    Addressing AI Challenges: Speed and Quality.......53
    Future Enhancements and Integrations..................55

Chapter Six: Gemini's Role on Google Pixel 9........ 60
    Gemini as the Default Assistant.............................60
    Long-Term Vision for AI-Powered Assistance........ 64

Conclusion.. 69

Introduction

In the fast-paced digital age, the role of personal assistants has evolved significantly. Digital assistants have transitioned from simple tools that set timers and play music to more sophisticated entities capable of managing various aspects of our lives. These advancements have been driven by the increasing need for efficiency and the quest to streamline daily tasks. As technology continues to advance, so too does the potential for digital assistants to become more integral to our daily routines.

Overview of Digital Assistants

Digital assistants, often powered by artificial intelligence (AI), have revolutionized the way we interact with technology. Initially, these assistants were designed to perform basic tasks such as setting reminders, sending messages, or providing weather updates. Examples of early digital assistants include Apple's Siri, Google's Assistant, and Amazon's Alexa. These tools were primarily built on predefined commands and scripts, which limited their ability to understand and respond to more complex requests.

Over time, digital assistants have grown more sophisticated. Advances in machine learning and natural language processing (NLP) have enabled them to understand context, interpret user intentions, and provide more relevant and personalized responses. This evolution has been marked by the integration of voice recognition technologies, which have allowed users to interact with their assistants more naturally and conversationally. Despite these improvements, traditional digital assistants still face limitations, particularly when handling multifaceted tasks or engaging in extended, context-rich dialogues.

The Evolution with Generative AI

The emergence of generative AI has marked a significant milestone in the evolution of digital assistants. Unlike earlier models that relied on pre-programmed responses, generative AI systems can create original content and responses based on a deep understanding of language patterns and context. This advancement is largely due to the development of sophisticated models such as OpenAI's GPT-3 and Google's Bard, which are designed to generate human-like text and engage in complex conversations.

Generative AI has transformed digital assistants by enhancing their ability to handle a broader range of tasks and provide more nuanced responses. For example, these models can now draft emails, generate creative content, and even offer detailed explanations on a variety of subjects. The technology leverages vast amounts of data and advanced algorithms to predict and generate responses that are contextually appropriate and relevant to the user's needs.

One of the key benefits of generative AI is its ability to engage in more dynamic and adaptive conversations. Unlike traditional models that may struggle with context-switching or handling interruptions, generative AI can maintain coherent dialogues, understand subtleties in language, and offer tailored assistance. This has opened up new possibilities for digital assistants to act as more than just task managers but as interactive partners that can support users in creative and strategic thinking.

Introducing Gemini: A New Level of Assistance

Amidst this backdrop of technological advancement, Gemini represents a significant leap forward in the realm of AI-powered personal assistance. Gemini is designed to leverage the capabilities of generative AI to offer a more intuitive and versatile assistant experience. With its latest features and innovations, Gemini aims to redefine what it means for a digital assistant to be genuinely helpful.

Gemini Live is one of the standout features of this new offering. It enables users to engage in free-flowing conversations with the assistant, making it possible to explore ideas, brainstorm solutions, or rehearse important conversations in a more interactive manner. Unlike traditional digital assistants, Gemini Live supports interruptions and allows users to pause and resume conversations, making it a powerful tool for dynamic and ongoing dialogues. This feature is particularly useful for tasks that require iterative thinking or detailed exploration, such as planning a project or preparing for a presentation.

In addition to Gemini Live, the integration of generative AI has allowed Gemini to connect seamlessly with a variety of Google apps and services. This includes advanced features for managing tasks, organizing information, and even creating personalized content. For example, users can ask Gemini to retrieve a recipe from an email, add ingredients to a shopping list, and create a music playlist—all within a single interaction. This level of integration reduces the need for users to switch between apps and streamline their workflows.

Another notable advancement is the enhanced contextual awareness of Gemini on Android devices. By integrating deeply with the Android user experience, Gemini can provide contextually relevant assistance based on the content currently on the screen. This includes the ability to interact with other apps and offer insights or actions related to the user's activities. For instance, Gemini can help users extract information from videos, draft messages, and more, all without leaving the current application.

Gemini also addresses some of the challenges associated with generative AI by introducing improvements in speed and response quality. The deployment of models like Gemini 1.5 Flash is aimed at enhancing the performance of the assistant, ensuring that responses are both timely and accurate. This focus on performance is crucial for maintaining user trust and ensuring that the assistant remains a reliable tool for managing various tasks.

However, the introduction of Gemini marks a significant advancement in the field of digital assistants. By leveraging the power of generative AI, Gemini offers a more conversational, context-aware, and integrated experience. As digital assistants continue to evolve, the capabilities demonstrated by Gemini set a new standard for what users can expect from their AI-powered assistants. With its innovative features and ongoing improvements, Gemini is poised to become a valuable tool in managing and enhancing daily life.

Chapter One

Gemini Live

Free-Flowing Conversations with Gemini

The introduction of Gemini Live represents a groundbreaking advancement in conversational AI, setting a new standard for how digital assistants interact with users. Traditional digital assistants have often been constrained by rigid command structures and predefined responses, limiting their ability to engage in natural, dynamic dialogues. Gemini Live, however, is designed to overcome these limitations by enabling free-flowing, interactive conversations that closely mimic human interaction.

With Gemini Live, users can engage in conversations that are not only contextually rich but also adaptable. This means that users can start a conversation about one topic, shift to another, and then return to the original subject without losing coherence. For example, if you are brainstorming ideas for a new project, you might initially discuss potential approaches, then switch to evaluating specific tools, and later revisit earlier ideas with new insights. Gemini Live handles these transitions seamlessly, maintaining the context and continuity of the discussion.

One of the key features of Gemini Live is its ability to handle interruptions. Users can ask follow-up questions or delve deeper into specific aspects of the conversation without disrupting the flow. This is particularly useful for complex tasks that require iterative exploration or detailed explanation. Unlike earlier models that might require users to restart a query or provide additional context, Gemini Live can adjust its responses in real time, offering a more fluid and engaging conversational experience.

The conversational capabilities of Gemini Live are underpinned by advanced natural language processing and machine learning technologies. These technologies enable the assistant to understand and generate human-like text, interpret nuances in user input, and provide relevant responses. This results in a more intuitive interaction where users can communicate their needs and ideas more naturally, without having to navigate through a rigid set of commands or options.

Hands-Free Operation and Background Use

Another significant enhancement offered by Gemini Live is its support for hands-free operation and background use. In contrast to traditional digital assistants, which often require users to actively engage with the device, Gemini Live allows for a more passive and continuous interaction. This hands-free capability is achieved through advanced voice recognition and background processing technologies.

Users can interact with Gemini Live even when their device is locked or when they are performing other tasks. For instance, if you are cooking and need to keep track of a recipe or manage a shopping list, you can continue speaking to Gemini Live without having to interact directly with your phone. This continuous engagement is facilitated by the assistant's ability to process voice commands and provide responses without requiring active input from the user.

The hands-free functionality also extends to situations where users are on the move. Whether you are walking, driving, or multitasking, you can maintain a conversation with Gemini Live as if you were on a phone call. This seamless integration into various activities allows for a more flexible and convenient user experience. The ability to interact with Gemini

Live in a hands-free manner not only enhances productivity but also ensures that users can stay engaged with their tasks without interruption.

Furthermore, the background use feature enables Gemini Live to provide timely assistance without disrupting the user's current activities. For example, if you are watching a video and have a question about its content, you can ask Gemini Live without pausing or exiting the video. The assistant can process your request, provide the information you need, and then allow you to continue with your viewing experience. This level of integration ensures that users can access assistance naturally and unobtrusively.

Availability: Rollout Schedule and Supported Platforms

The rollout of Gemini Live is designed to bring this advanced conversational experience to a wide range of users across different platforms. Initially, Gemini Live is being introduced to Android users, with the rollout starting today for English-speaking Gemini Advanced subscribers. This phased approach allows for gradual adoption and ensures that the feature is refined based on user feedback.

In the coming weeks, Gemini Live will expand to iOS users, broadening its availability to a wider audience. This cross-platform support ensures that users on both Android and iOS devices can benefit from the enhanced conversational capabilities of Gemini Live. The expansion to additional languages is also planned, making the feature accessible to a global user base and accommodating diverse linguistic needs.

The rollout schedule for Gemini Live reflects a strategic approach to introducing new features while maintaining a focus on quality and user experience. By initially releasing the feature to a select group of users, the development team can monitor performance, address any issues, and gather valuable insights to inform future updates. This iterative approach ensures that the final release is well-optimized and meets the expectations of a broader audience.

Overall, Gemini Live represents a significant advancement in the field of conversational AI. Its ability to support free-flowing conversations, hands-free operation, and background use sets a new standard for digital assistants. The gradual rollout and platform support ensure that users across different devices and regions will have the opportunity to experience these innovative features. As Gemini Live continues to evolve, it is poised to redefine how users interact with their digital assistants, offering a more natural, engaging, and productive experience.

Chapter Two

New Voice Options

Selecting the Best Voice to Meet Your Needs

The advancement of voice technology has become a cornerstone of modern digital assistants, significantly enhancing user experience by allowing for a more personalized and engaging interaction. Gemini's latest update introduces a range of new voice options, offering users the ability to select a voice that best fits their preferences and needs. This feature represents a shift towards greater customization and user-centric design in the realm of conversational AI.

Choosing the right voice for your digital assistant can significantly impact the quality and enjoyment of interactions. Different voices can convey varying tones, styles, and levels of formality, which can affect how users perceive and engage with the assistant. For instance, a more conversational and friendly voice might make interactions feel more personal and approachable, while a professional and authoritative tone might be preferable for business-related tasks.

Gemini's new voice options are designed to cater to a diverse range of preferences and use cases. Users can select from multiple voices that vary in gender, accent, and speaking style. This level of customization allows users to align the assistant's voice with their tastes or the specific context in which they are using the assistant. For example, a user might prefer a calming voice for daily reminders and relaxation activities, while a more energetic voice might be suited for dynamic tasks and brainstorming sessions.

Additionally, the ability to choose a voice can enhance accessibility and inclusivity. For users with hearing impairments or those who are non-native speakers, having the option to select a voice that is easier to understand or more comfortable to listen to can make a significant difference in the effectiveness and ease of interaction. This personalization helps ensure that the assistant can serve a broader audience, accommodating various needs and preferences.

The process of selecting a voice is typically straightforward, involving a simple configuration within the Gemini app. Users can listen to samples of each voice option before making a selection, allowing them to choose the voice that best aligns with their preferences. This feature empowers users to customize their experience and interact with the assistant in a way that feels natural and engaging.

Demonstration of Voice Features

The demonstration of voice features within Gemini highlights the advancements in voice technology and how they contribute to a more immersive and effective user experience. By offering a variety of voices and demonstrating their capabilities, Gemini showcases the potential for voice customization to enhance interactions and provide tailored support.

One of the key features demonstrated is the ability to switch between different voices during a conversation. This functionality allows users to experience how each voice performs in real-time, helping them make an informed choice about which voice best suits their needs. For instance, users might test how a particular voice handles various types of queries, such as providing weather updates, setting reminders, or answering complex questions. This practical demonstration provides insight into how each voice performs in different scenarios and helps users select the most suitable option.

Another important aspect of the voice features demonstration is the emphasis on naturalness and clarity. The new voices are designed to be more expressive and lifelike, with improved intonation and modulation. This enhancement contributes to a more engaging and realistic interaction, making it easier for users to connect with the assistant on a personal level. The demonstration might include examples of how the voice handles different emotional tones, such as enthusiasm or empathy, and how it adjusts to various conversational contexts.

The demonstration also highlights the versatility of the new voices in handling different languages and accents. Gemini's voices are designed to accommodate a range of linguistic and cultural nuances, providing users with a more authentic and relatable experience. For example, users can experience how the voice adapts to regional accents or handles multilingual queries, showcasing the assistant's ability to cater to a global audience.

Additionally, the demonstration of voice features often includes examples of the voice's responsiveness and accuracy. Users can observe how quickly and effectively the assistant responds to commands or questions, as well as how well it maintains coherence and context throughout a conversation. This aspect of the demonstration is crucial for ensuring that users can rely on the assistant to provide timely and accurate information.

Overall, the introduction of new voice options and the demonstration of their features mark a significant advancement in the field of conversational AI. By offering a diverse range of voices and showcasing their capabilities, Gemini enhances the user experience and provides greater customization and personalization. The ability to choose a voice that aligns with individual preferences and needs not only makes interactions more enjoyable but also helps ensure that the assistant is more effective and accessible to a wider audience.

As voice technology continues to evolve, the focus on personalization and user-centric design will likely play an increasingly important role. Gemini's new voice options represent a step forward in this direction, offering users the tools they need to create a more tailored and engaging interaction with their digital assistant. With these advancements, users can look forward to a more customized and satisfying experience, making their interactions with Gemini both effective and enjoyable.

Chapter Three

App Integration and Extensions

Seamless Integration with Google Apps

One of the standout features of Gemini is its seamless integration with Google Apps, a capability that significantly enhances its functionality and user experience. This integration is designed to streamline workflows and simplify task management by allowing users to interact with multiple Google services through a single interface. By leveraging the interconnectedness of Google's ecosystem,

Gemini can provide a more cohesive and efficient user experience.

When Gemini integrates with Google Apps, it enables users to perform a wide range of tasks without needing to switch between different applications. For example, users can manage their emails, calendar events, and notes all within the Gemini platform, creating a unified workspace that reduces the need for context-switching. This integration not only saves time but also ensures that users can access and manage their information more efficiently.

The seamless nature of this integration means that Gemini can pull information from various Google Apps and use it to provide contextually relevant assistance. For instance, if a user asks Gemini to find a document or email, the assistant can search across Google Drive or Gmail, pulling up relevant results based on the user's query. This capability enhances the accuracy and relevance of the information provided, making it easier for users to locate and utilize their data.

Moreover, the integration extends to Google's suite of productivity tools, such as Google Sheets and Google Docs. Users can interact with these tools through Gemini, making it possible to perform tasks like editing documents, creating spreadsheets, and tracking project progress without leaving the assistant's interface. This level of integration simplifies complex workflows and allows users to stay focused on their tasks without needing to navigate through multiple apps.

Managing Tasks with Gemini

Gemini's ability to manage tasks effectively is one of its core strengths, and this functionality is significantly enhanced by its integration with Google's productivity tools. Two key features in this regard are the integration with Google Keep and Google Tasks, which provide users with powerful tools for managing their to-do lists, notes, and reminders.

Keep and Tasks Integration

Google Keep is a versatile note-taking app that allows users to capture and organize ideas, tasks, and reminders. By integrating with Google Keep, Gemini can offer users a more streamlined way to manage their notes and lists. Users can ask Gemini to add items to their Keep notes, create new lists, or retrieve information from existing notes. For example, if a user wants to add a new grocery item to their shopping list, they can simply tell Gemini to add it to their Keep list, and the assistant will handle the update automatically.

Similarly, Google Tasks is a task management app that helps users keep track of their to-dos and deadlines. Gemini's integration with Google Tasks allows users to manage their tasks directly through the assistant. Users can create new tasks, set deadlines, and mark tasks as complete without needing to open the Google Tasks app. This integration provides a convenient way for users to stay on top of their responsibilities and ensures that their task lists are always up-to-date.

The integration with these tools means that users can manage their notes and tasks more efficiently, with Gemini acting as a central hub for task management. This functionality is particularly useful for users who need to juggle multiple responsibilities and want a streamlined way to keep track of their progress.

YouTube Music Features

Another area where Gemini's integration shines is in its interaction with YouTube Music. As a popular music streaming service, YouTube Music offers a vast library of songs, albums, and playlists. Gemini's integration with YouTube Music allows users to manage their music experience through the assistant, making it easier to discover, organize, and play their favorite tunes.

Users can ask Gemini to create new playlists, add songs to existing playlists, or play specific tracks from YouTube Music. For example, if a user is hosting a dinner party and wants to set the mood with a playlist of relaxing music, they can simply ask Gemini to create a new playlist and add suitable tracks. The assistant can also help users find music based on specific themes, moods, or genres, making it easier to curate the perfect listening experience.

The integration also allows for more personalized recommendations. By analyzing user preferences and listening habits, Gemini can suggest new music or playlists that align with the user's tastes. This level of personalization enhances the user experience and helps users discover new content that they might enjoy.

Calendar Extension: Scheduling and Reminders

The calendar extension is another powerful feature of Gemini, providing users with a comprehensive tool for managing their schedules and setting reminders. This extension integrates with Google Calendar to offer a range of scheduling and reminder functionalities that help users stay organized and on top of their commitments.

With the calendar extension, users can interact with their calendars directly through Gemini. For instance, users can ask Gemini to check their availability for a specific date, add new events, or modify existing ones. This functionality simplifies the process of managing appointments and ensures that users can keep their schedules up-to-date without needing to navigate through multiple calendar interfaces.

The extension also allows users to set reminders for important events or deadlines. Users can ask Gemini to remind them about upcoming meetings, deadlines, or tasks, ensuring that they stay on track with their responsibilities. The ability to set reminders through the assistant makes it easier for users to manage their time effectively and ensures that they never miss important dates or commitments.

Furthermore, Gemini's calendar extension can handle more complex scheduling tasks, such as coordinating events with multiple participants. Users can ask Gemini to schedule meetings, send invites, and manage RSVPs, streamlining the process of organizing group events and ensuring that all participants are informed and prepared.

However, Gemini's app integration and extensions provide a powerful set of tools for managing productivity and enhancing user experience. By seamlessly integrating with Google Apps, users can streamline their workflows and access a unified interface for managing their notes, tasks, music, and calendar events. The ability to interact with these tools through Gemini makes it easier to stay organized, manage responsibilities, and enjoy a more personalized and efficient digital experience.

Chapter Four

Enhanced Android Integration

Context-Aware Capabilities on Android

The enhanced integration of Gemini with Android brings a significant leap in context-aware capabilities, revolutionizing how users interact with their devices. Context-awareness refers to a digital assistant's ability to understand and adapt to the current environment and user activity, providing more relevant and timely assistance. With Gemini's advanced integration into Android, this capability is taken to new heights, enabling a more intuitive and seamless user experience.

On Android, Gemini is designed to be highly context-aware, meaning it can respond to user needs based on the current activity or app in use. This is achieved through deep integration with the Android operating system, allowing Gemini to access and interpret information from various sources in real time. For instance, if you're reading an email and need to quickly check your calendar, Gemini can provide a summary of your upcoming appointments without requiring you to switch apps or manually search for the information.

Context-aware capabilities extend to various scenarios. For example, if you're watching a video on YouTube and have a question about the content, Gemini can offer relevant information or summarize key points without interrupting your viewing experience. Similarly, while using a navigation app, Gemini can offer insights or answer questions related to your route, enhancing the overall efficiency of your journey.

The integration also enables Gemini to adapt to different usage patterns and preferences. By learning from your interactions and understanding your habits, Gemini can provide personalized recommendations and support. This could involve suggesting shortcuts based on frequently used apps or offering contextual reminders based on recent activities. The ability to tailor responses and actions to the current context ensures that Gemini remains a valuable tool for enhancing productivity and convenience.

Interacting with Content on Your Screen

One of the standout features of Gemini's enhanced Android integration is its ability to interact with the content currently displayed on your screen. This functionality allows Gemini to offer more precise and relevant assistance based on the specific content you're viewing or working with at any given moment.

For example, if you're browsing a website and come across a piece of information you want to learn more about, you can ask Gemini for additional details or related content without needing to leave the page. This interaction is facilitated by Gemini's ability to analyze and understand the content on your screen, providing responses that are directly relevant to your current activity.

Similarly, while using productivity apps like Google Docs or Sheets, Gemini can assist with tasks such as drafting content, performing calculations, or organizing data. If you're working on a document and need to reference specific information or add new content, Gemini can offer suggestions or help with editing in real time. This level of interaction ensures that you can stay focused on your work while receiving timely support from the assistant.

The ability to interact with screen content also extends to providing actionable insights. For instance, if you're viewing a travel itinerary, Gemini can offer recommendations for nearby attractions or restaurants based on your location. This contextual assistance enhances the value of the information displayed on your screen, making it more useful and actionable.

Overall, the integration of Gemini with Android's screen content interaction capabilities adds a layer of convenience and efficiency to the user experience. By providing relevant assistance based on what's currently being viewed or worked on, Gemini ensures that users can access the support they need without disrupting their workflow or navigation.

Drag-and-Drop Functionality

Another significant enhancement in Gemini's Android integration is the introduction of drag-and-drop functionality. This feature allows users to easily move and manage content across different apps and interfaces using simple drag-and-drop gestures. The incorporation of drag-and-drop functionality into Gemini's ecosystem streamlines interactions and enhances overall productivity.

For example, if Gemini generates an image or document that you want to include in an email or message, you can simply drag and drop the content into the relevant application. This eliminates the need for cumbersome copy-pasting or saving files before sharing them. Whether you're transferring images, text, or other types of content, the drag-and-drop feature facilitates a smoother and more intuitive process.

This functionality is particularly useful for tasks that involve handling multiple types of content simultaneously. For instance, if you're creating a presentation and need to incorporate information from various sources, you can drag and drop text or images from Gemini directly into your presentation slides. This capability reduces the time spent switching between apps and enhances the efficiency of content management.

Drag-and-drop functionality also enhances the ease of organizing and managing files and data. Users can quickly rearrange items within an app or between different apps, making it easier to organize their information and keep their workflows streamlined. For example, if you're managing a project and need to move files between a project management app and a cloud storage service, you can do so with minimal effort using drag-and-drop gestures.

Moreover, the integration of drag-and-drop functionality into Gemini's Android experience reflects a broader trend towards more tactile and interactive user interfaces. By leveraging familiar gestures and interactions, Gemini enhances the user experience and aligns with the intuitive design principles of modern mobile operating systems.

However, Gemini's enhanced Android integration brings a host of benefits that significantly improve the user experience. The context-aware capabilities ensure that the assistant provides timely and relevant assistance based on current activities, while the ability to interact with screen content allows for more precise support. Additionally, the introduction of drag-and-drop functionality streamlines content management and enhances productivity. Together, these features make

Gemini a powerful tool for optimizing mobile interactions and enhancing overall efficiency on Android devices.

Chapter Five

Performance Improvements

Introduction of Gemini 1.5 Flash

In the rapidly evolving landscape of artificial intelligence, performance improvements are crucial for maintaining relevance and delivering exceptional user experiences. Gemini 1.5 Flash represents a significant milestone in this ongoing quest for excellence. This new iteration of Gemini's AI model is designed to address key performance issues and enhance the overall effectiveness of the digital assistant.

Gemini 1.5 Flash introduces several advancements over its predecessors, focusing on improving both speed and response quality. One of the most notable enhancements is the model's increased processing speed. Gemini 1.5 Flash leverages cutting-edge computational techniques to accelerate response times, ensuring that users receive answers and assistance more swiftly. This improvement is particularly important in contexts where timely information is critical, such as managing tasks, responding to inquiries, or navigating complex workflows.

Another key feature of Gemini 1.5 Flash is its enhanced ability to handle complex queries and provide more accurate and nuanced responses. The model has been trained on a diverse dataset, allowing it to better understand and interpret a wide range of questions and requests. This enhanced understanding translates into more relevant and contextually appropriate responses, improving the overall quality of interactions with the assistant.

The introduction of Gemini 1.5 Flash also involves optimizations in the underlying architecture of the AI model. These optimizations contribute to a more efficient use of computational resources, reducing latency and ensuring that the assistant operates smoothly even under high demand. This advancement not only benefits individual users but also supports the scalability of the assistant, allowing it to handle a growing number of interactions and requests.

Addressing AI Challenges: Speed and Quality

The pursuit of performance improvements in AI, particularly in digital assistants like Gemini, involves tackling several key challenges, most notably speed and quality. Achieving a balance between these two aspects is essential for delivering a satisfactory user experience and ensuring that the assistant meets diverse needs effectively.

Speed is a critical factor in user satisfaction. In the context of digital assistants, slow response times can lead to frustration and diminished productivity. Gemini 1.5 Flash addresses this challenge by incorporating advanced algorithms and optimization techniques that enhance processing speed. By reducing the time it takes for the assistant to generate and deliver responses, Gemini 1.5 Flash ensures that users can access the information and assistance they need without unnecessary delays.

However, speed alone is not sufficient. **The quality** of responses is equally important. Users expect digital assistants to provide accurate, relevant, and contextually appropriate information. Achieving high-quality responses involves several components, including advanced natural language processing, robust training datasets, and a sophisticated understanding of user intent. Gemini 1.5 Flash enhances response quality by leveraging improved machine-learning models that are better equipped to handle nuanced and complex queries. The model's ability to provide detailed and accurate answers enhances its overall usefulness and reliability.

The challenge of balancing speed and quality is further compounded by the need for continuous learning and adaptation. As user interactions generate new data and insights, the AI model must evolve to incorporate this information and improve its performance over time. Gemini 1.5 Flash addresses this challenge through iterative updates and refinements, ensuring that the assistant remains effective and relevant as user needs and expectations change.

Future Enhancements and Integrations

Looking ahead, the development of Gemini is set to continue evolving with a focus on future enhancements and integrations. These advancements will build on the improvements introduced with Gemini 1.5 Flash and aim to further elevate the capabilities of the digital assistant.

Future Enhancements will likely include advancements in natural language understanding and generation, enabling Gemini to handle increasingly complex and diverse queries with greater ease. As AI research progresses, new techniques and models will be integrated into Gemini to enhance its ability to understand context, interpret user intent, and provide more sophisticated responses. These enhancements will contribute to a more intuitive and responsive user experience, making the assistant even more valuable and versatile.

Integrations will play a crucial role in expanding Gemini's functionality and ensuring that it can effectively support a wide range of tasks and applications. Future integrations are expected to include deeper connections with third-party apps and services, allowing Gemini to interact seamlessly with a broader ecosystem of tools and platforms. For example, integrations with productivity apps, communication platforms, and smart home devices will enable users to manage their entire digital environment through a unified interface.

Additionally, Gemini's integration with emerging technologies such as augmented reality (AR) and virtual reality (VR) could open new possibilities for interactive and immersive experiences. By leveraging these technologies, Gemini could provide context-aware assistance in virtual environments, enhance remote collaboration, and offer new ways for users to engage with digital content.

The ongoing focus on performance improvements will also involve refining the underlying infrastructure to support increased scalability and reliability. As the number of users and interactions grows, ensuring that Gemini can handle high volumes of requests without compromising performance will be a key priority. Investments in server infrastructure, data management, and optimization will support the continued growth and effectiveness of the assistant.

However, the introduction of Gemini 1.5 Flash marks a significant advancement in the evolution of the digital assistant, addressing key challenges related to speed and quality. By enhancing processing speed and response accuracy, Gemini 1.5 Flash sets a new standard for performance in AI-driven assistance. Looking to the future, ongoing enhancements and integrations will further expand Gemini's capabilities, ensuring that it remains a valuable and effective tool for users across a range of applications. The commitment to continuous improvement and innovation positions Gemini at the forefront of digital assistant technology, ready to meet the evolving needs of its users.

Chapter Six

Gemini's Role on Google Pixel 9

Gemini as the Default Assistant

The integration of Gemini as the default assistant on the Google Pixel 9 represents a significant step in the evolution of AI-powered assistance. By making Gemini the primary digital assistant on this flagship device, Google aims to enhance user experience through advanced AI capabilities and seamless integration with the Android ecosystem. This move highlights Gemini's growing prominence and the role it plays in shaping the future of mobile technology.

As the default assistant, Gemini becomes the central hub for managing various tasks and interactions on the Google Pixel 9. Users can rely on Gemini for a wide range of functions, from setting reminders and managing schedules to answering questions and controlling smart home devices. The decision to make Gemini the default assistant underscores Google's commitment to providing a comprehensive and intuitive AI experience that is deeply integrated into the device's core functionalities.

One of the key advantages of having Gemini as the default assistant is its ability to offer a more personalized and cohesive experience. Gemini's deep integration with the Pixel 9's hardware and software allows it to leverage the device's capabilities to provide tailored assistance. For example, Gemini can utilize the Pixel 9's advanced camera features to offer context-aware suggestions or assist with tasks like image recognition and processing. This level of integration ensures that users receive the most relevant and useful support based on the specific features and functions of their device.

Moreover, by making Gemini the default assistant, Google aims to streamline user interactions and reduce the friction associated with switching between different apps and services. Users can access Gemini's assistance directly from the home screen, lock screen, or through voice commands, providing a seamless and efficient way to manage tasks and access information. This convenience enhances the overall user experience, making it easier for users to interact with their devices and accomplish their goals.

The role of Gemini as the default assistant also reflects a broader trend towards consolidating digital assistant functionalities into a single, cohesive platform. As more devices and services become interconnected, having a unified assistant that can manage and coordinate various aspects of digital life becomes increasingly valuable. Gemini's integration into the Google Pixel 9 exemplifies this trend, offering a streamlined and integrated approach to AI-powered assistance.

Long-Term Vision for AI-Powered Assistance

The introduction of Gemini as the default assistant on the Google Pixel 9 is part of a broader long-term vision for the future of AI-powered assistance. This vision encompasses several key areas, including enhanced personalization, seamless integration across devices, and the development of new capabilities that leverage emerging technologies.

Enhanced Personalization is a central focus of the long-term vision for AI-powered assistance. As AI technology continues to advance, the ability to tailor interactions and responses to individual users becomes increasingly important. Gemini's integration into the Pixel 9 is designed to provide a highly personalized experience by learning from user interactions and preferences. Over time, Gemini will be able to offer more relevant suggestions, anticipate user needs, and provide tailored assistance based on individual habits and preferences. This level of personalization enhances the value of the assistant and ensures that it remains a valuable tool for users.

Seamless Integration Across Devices is another crucial aspect of the long-term vision. As users increasingly interact with multiple devices, from smartphones and tablets to smart home systems and wearables, having a unified assistant that can seamlessly integrate across these platforms becomes essential. Gemini's role on the Google Pixel 9 is just one part of this broader strategy. By extending its capabilities to other Google devices and services, Gemini aims to provide a consistent and integrated experience across the entire digital ecosystem. This integration ensures that users can access the same level of assistance and support, regardless of the device they are using.

Development of New Capabilities is also a key component of the long-term vision for AI-powered assistance. As AI technology continues to evolve, new opportunities for enhancing functionality and user experience emerge. Gemini's future developments are expected to include advancements in natural language processing, contextual understanding, and interaction capabilities. For example, future updates may enable Gemini to handle more complex and nuanced queries, provide more sophisticated recommendations, and integrate with emerging technologies such as augmented reality (AR) and virtual reality (VR).

These advancements will further expand the range of tasks and interactions that Gemini can support, enhancing its overall value and utility.

Ethical Considerations and user privacy are also important aspects of the long-term vision for AI-powered assistance. As AI technology becomes more integrated into daily life, ensuring that user data is handled responsibly and transparently becomes increasingly important. Google is committed to addressing these concerns by implementing robust privacy and security measures, ensuring that users can interact with Gemini with confidence. This commitment to ethical considerations reinforces the trust and reliability of the assistant, making it a more valuable and trusted tool for users.

However, the role of Gemini as the default assistant on the Google Pixel 9 marks a significant milestone in the evolution of AI-powered assistance. By offering a highly integrated and personalized experience, Gemini enhances the value and functionality of the Pixel 9, providing users with a streamlined and efficient way to manage their digital lives. The long-term vision for AI-powered assistance encompasses enhanced personalization, seamless integration across devices, and the development of new capabilities, all of which contribute to a more intuitive and valuable user experience. As AI technology continues to advance, Gemini's role as a central component of Google's digital ecosystem will continue to evolve, shaping the future of AI-powered assistance and transforming the way users interact with their devices.

Conclusion

The future of AI-powered assistants is poised to be transformative, shaping how we interact with technology and manage our daily lives. As artificial intelligence continues to evolve, so too will the capabilities and functionalities of digital assistants like Gemini. The trajectory of AI assistants points towards a future where they become even more integral to our personal and professional lives, offering a blend of efficiency, personalization, and intelligent automation.

Enhanced Intelligence and Capabilities will be a cornerstone of the future of AI-powered assistants. As machine learning models and natural language processing technologies advance, AI assistants will become increasingly adept at understanding complex queries and providing nuanced responses. This progress will enable them to handle a broader range of tasks with greater accuracy and relevance. For instance, future AI assistants might not only answer questions but also predict needs based on user behavior and contextual cues, offering proactive support and solutions.

Integration with Emerging Technologies is another significant aspect of the future landscape. AI assistants are expected to seamlessly interact with a growing array of devices and platforms, from smart home systems to wearable tech and augmented reality environments. This expanded integration will enhance the assistant's ability to manage and coordinate activities across different contexts, providing a more cohesive and interconnected user experience. For example, an AI assistant could integrate with AR glasses to offer real-time guidance and information in various scenarios, or with smart home systems to automate and optimize daily routines.

Increased Personalization will also play a crucial role in the future of AI assistants. As these systems become more sophisticated, they will be able to tailor interactions and responses to individual users with greater precision. This level of personalization will be driven by advances in data analysis and machine learning, allowing AI assistants to learn from user preferences, habits, and feedback. As a result, users will experience more relevant recommendations, customized assistance, and a deeper understanding of their needs.

Ethical Considerations and Privacy will be paramount as AI assistants become more embedded in everyday life. Ensuring that user data is handled securely and transparently will be essential for maintaining trust and ensuring responsible use of AI technology. Future developments will likely include enhanced privacy controls and ethical guidelines to address these concerns, ensuring that AI assistants operate within frameworks that prioritize user security and ethical considerations.

AI-driven innovation will also continue to push the boundaries of what is possible with digital assistants. As new technologies and applications emerge, AI assistants will evolve to incorporate these advancements, offering innovative features and capabilities that enhance their utility and effectiveness. This ongoing innovation will drive the evolution of AI assistants, making them increasingly valuable tools for users across various domains.

User Expectations and Continuous Improvement

As AI-powered assistants like Gemini advance, user expectations will continue to evolve, driving the need for continuous improvement and innovation. Understanding and addressing these expectations will be crucial for maintaining user satisfaction and ensuring that AI assistants meet the diverse needs of their audiences.

Expectations for Accuracy and Relevance will be high as users increasingly rely on AI assistants for critical tasks and information. Users expect AI assistants to provide accurate, timely, and contextually relevant responses. To meet these expectations, ongoing improvements in natural language processing, machine learning algorithms, and data integration will be necessary. AI assistants must be able to interpret and respond to complex queries with precision, ensuring that users receive reliable and useful assistance.

Ease of Use and Accessibility will also be key factors in user expectations. As AI assistants become more integral to daily life, users will expect them to be intuitive and easy to interact with. This includes seamless integration with various devices and platforms, as well as user-friendly interfaces that facilitate efficient interactions. Continuous refinement of user interfaces and interaction models will be essential for meeting these expectations and ensuring that AI assistants remain accessible and user-friendly.

Personalization and Customization will be increasingly important as users seek more tailored and relevant experiences. AI assistants will need to adapt to individual preferences and habits, offering personalized recommendations and support that align with users' unique needs and goals. This level of personalization will require sophisticated data analysis and machine learning capabilities, enabling AI assistants to learn and evolve based on user interactions and feedback.

Trust and Transparency will be critical in maintaining user confidence in AI assistants. Users will expect clear communication about how their data is used and how AI decisions are made. Building and maintaining trust will involve implementing robust privacy measures, providing transparent information about data usage, and ensuring that AI systems operate ethically and responsibly. Ongoing efforts to address privacy concerns and ethical considerations will be essential for sustaining user trust and satisfaction.

Adaptability and Innovation will be necessary to keep pace with changing user needs and technological advancements. As new applications and technologies emerge, AI assistants must evolve and integrate these innovations to remain relevant and effective. Continuous development and adaptation will ensure that AI assistants meet evolving user expectations and provide valuable support across diverse contexts.

In conclusion, the future of AI-powered assistants holds tremendous potential for enhancing user experiences and transforming how we interact with technology. As these systems become more intelligent, integrated, and personalized, they will play an increasingly central role in managing our daily lives and activities. Meeting user expectations will require ongoing improvements in accuracy, ease of use, personalization, trust, and a commitment to ethical considerations and innovation. By addressing these factors and continuously evolving, AI assistants like Gemini will continue to advance, offering valuable support and shaping the future of digital interaction.

www.ingramcontent.com/pod-product-compliance
Lightning Source LLC
Chambersburg PA
CBHW070359230526
45471CB00006B/2641